FANTASTIC FLEXAGONS

Hexaflexagons and Other Flexible Folds to Twist and Turn

Nick Robinson

FOR YOUNG READERS

Racehorse for Young Readers books may be purchased in bulk at special discounts for sales promotion, corporate gifts, fund-raising, or educational purposes. Special editions can also be created to specifications. For details, contact the Special Sales Department, Skyhorse Publishing, 307 West 36th Street, 11th Floor, New York, NY 10018 or info@skyhorsepublishing.com.

Racehorse for Young Readers™ is a pending trademark of Skyhorse Publishing, Inc.®, a Delaware corporation.

Visit our website at www.skyhorsepublishing.com.

10 9 8 7 6 5 4 3 2

Text and folds by Nick Robinson
Cover design by Alexandra Rice and Joshua Seong
Interior layout by Alexandra Rice
Cover photos by Alexandra Rice
Produced by Karen Matsu Greenberg

Print ISBN: 978-1-944686-10-9

Printed in China

CONTENTS

Color and patterns disappear and re-appear again and again as flexagons twist, turn, and rotate. Flexagons are flat paper models that, when put through a series of flexes and folds, uncover and reveal hidden faces. Arthur Stone discovered them in 1939 while studying at Princeton University in New Jersey. From Great Britain, his binder was designed for English-sized paper (8.27in × 11.7in / 210mm x 297mm). To get his U.S.-sized paper (8.50in × 11in / 216mm s 279mm) to fit, he cut a short strip off at one end. Playing with the strips, he added 60-degree creases and before long, was looking at the first known 'flexagon'. He showed this to his colleagues (including Bryant Tuckerman, Richard P. Fenynman and John Tukey), and they established the *Princeton Flexagon Committee* developing a mathematical theory to explain how these mezmerizing papertoys flex.

From the trihexa-flexagon, it was discovered that the number of faces could be expanded simply by using a longer strip. Other designs included triangular, square, penta and even hexagon-based flexagons. The public first learned about Hexaflexagons from Martin Gardner In December 1956, when he sold an article about it to *Scientific American* magazine. In 1959 Gardner published "Mathematical Puzzles and Diversions", which continues to inspire people throughout the world over these many years.

In thinking about flexing, flipping and hidden faces, let's investigate the most basic example, a Möbius strip. Take a strip of paper and give it a half-twist; then join the ends of the strip to form a loop. If you trace a line along the middle of this strip, you will return to the starting point after traveling along the entire length of the strip without ever crossing an edge. Your finger will travel continuously on both sides of the paper, yet the two sides will never meet and always appear 'as one'. Möbius strips start us thinking about hidden and exposed faces.

Tri-tetra and Tetra-tetra are folds that help us understand basic Flexagon principals built from the simplest square shapes. When you reach the end of a series of flexes it is often necessary to reverse the process to get back to the other "end". Flippers are variations of flexagons that use glue and a few cuts to form shapes that will rotate endlessly around themselves.

Kaleidocycles are shapes formed by taking a number of tetrahedra and joining their edges to form a chain. The ends of the chain are then joined to form a ring. This ring can then be rotated so that it turns inside out indefinitely. The name comes from the Greek - kálos (beautiful) + eîdos (form) + kyklos (ring). It can be shown that whilst a ring of regular 60 degree tetrahedra will not flex, if one of their corners is extended slightly, it can indeed flex.

Together, all these form a set of shapes, both flat and 3D, that rotate to reveal hidden faces. It is not necessary to study their mathematical and geometric properties to enjoy the practical aspect of these fascinating designs.

To get started in creating really great Flexagons and Kaliedocycles, you'll want to keep these three things in mind: accurate cutting, sharp creasing, and accuracy of laying down glue. Start by clearing a work space and gather your clear tape, sharp scissors, and white glue. A straight edge may also be useful for making precise creases. For practice models, you may want to use double-side sticky tape instead of glue.

Read all of the fold instrucions and patterns (they progress from simpler to complex), and select the Flexagon pattern you want to create first. Carefully cut, crease, glue and tape the pattern per the instructions on the fold. Some of the patterned-pages (included), have more than one pattern. When gluing, start with one small dot of white glue in the center of the area-to-be-glued and use a toothpick or stick to spread the glue evenly over the indicated surface; then join to the corresponding side.

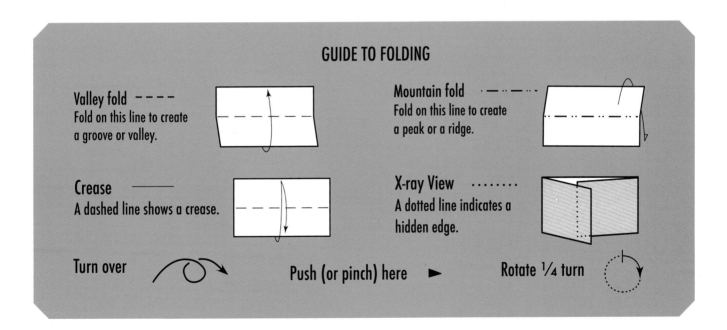

Flexing also has great benefits to your peace of mind – much like "worry beads", the smooth, repetitive process of flexing helps the mind to let go of troubling issues. Puzzling through the geometric forms that are revealed during a flex are intriguing, beautiful and meditative, and once you've got some of these models completed, take the time to properly appreciate them.

TRI-TETRA

This design has 3 faces and 4 edges. Interestingly, while you can see faces 1 & 2 and 1 & 3, there is no way to flex so that you can see the combination of faces 2 & 3.

1]

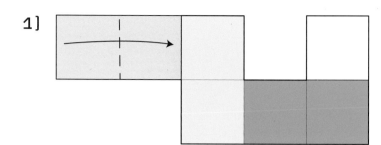

After cutting out the pattern, begin by folding the far-left square onto the adjacent square to the right.

2]

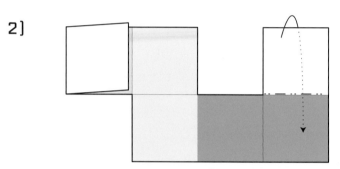

Now fold the top-right square down to the back.

3]

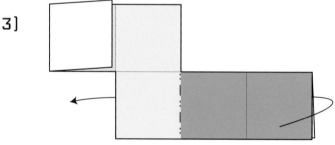

Fold back the lower two right squares, so that they go behind.

4]

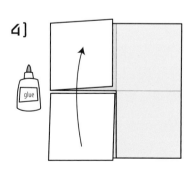

Fold the lower white square upwards and glue to the other white square.

5]

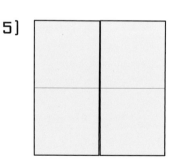

Complete.

FLEXING:

1]

Face 1. Turn the paper over.

2]

Face 2. Turn the paper over.

3]

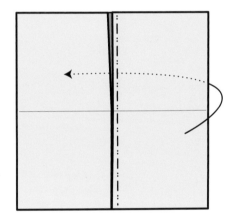

Fold the right half underneath.

4]

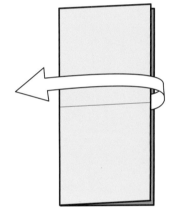

Separate the two layers and open the upper layer to the right.

5]

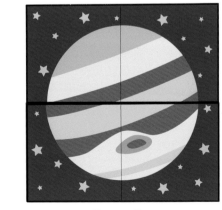

Face 3.

TETRA-TETRA

This design has 4 faces and 4 edges. Here, we use a small strip of tape to attach the end of the flexagon together.

1]

Begin by making a cut along the dotted line.

2]

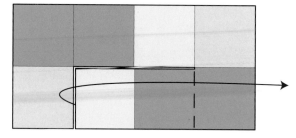

On the lower row, fold the two middle squares to the right.

3]

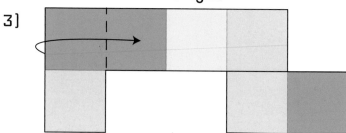

Fold the two vertical squares on the left column over to the right.

4]

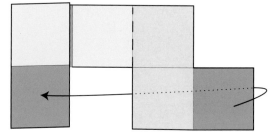

Fold under the 2 lower and 1 upper square on the right side and once folded, bring the right-most flap on top of the lower left square.

5]

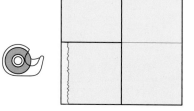

Tape the left edge of the bottom left square to complete.

FLEXING:

1]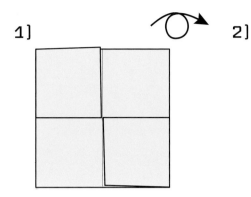

Face 1. Turn the paper over.

2]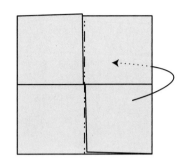

Face 2. Fold the right half underneath.

3]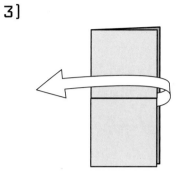

Lift up a flap on the right and open to the left.

4]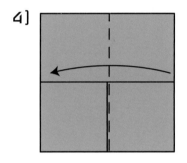

Face 3. Fold in half from right to left.

5]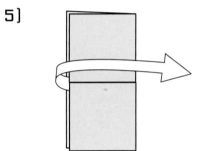

Lift up a flap on the left and open to the right.

6]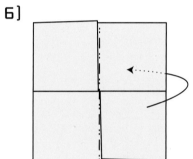

Face 1. Fold the right half underneath.

7]

Lift up a flap on the right and open to the left.

8]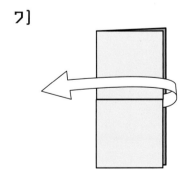

Face 4.

FLIPPER

You will find the flexing of this design to be unusual, unexpected but also intriguing. As with all flexagons, make the initial folding slowly and carefully until the creases learn how to fold.

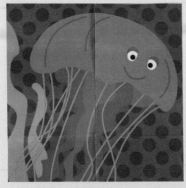

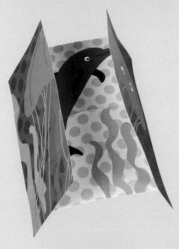

1]

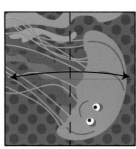 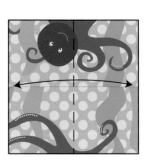

Begin with art positioned as shown on pattern pages. Crease in half from side to side and unfold.

2]

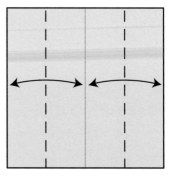

On both parts, fold the sides to the center, crease and unfold.

3]

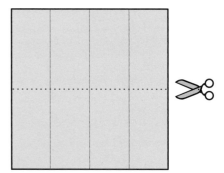

Cut along the horizontal center. Repeat with the second square. Turn both sheets over.

4]

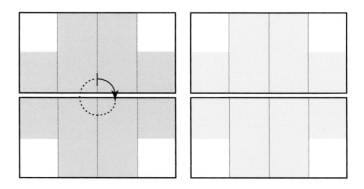

Rotate the fisrt sheets by 90 degrees to the right.

5]

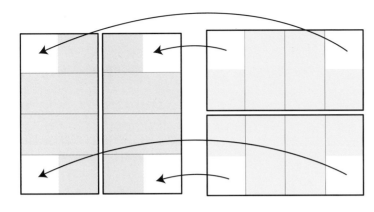

Carefully apply glue only to the white outside corners and arrange one square on top of the other. Hold in place while the glue dries.

6]

Complete. Turn over.

FLEXING:

1]

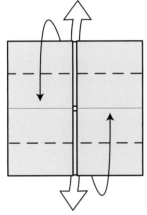

Fold top and bottom edges to the horizontal center, allowing layers to flip out from underneath.

2]

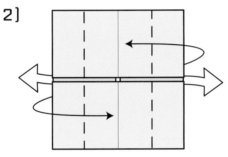

Fold left and right quarters into the vertical center.

3]

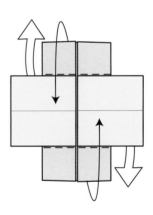

Fold top and bottom edges to the horizontal center, allowing layers to flip out from underneath.

4]

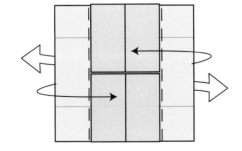

Fold the side flaps into the vertical center, allowing layers to flip out from behind.

5]

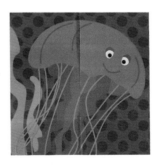

The cycle is complete.

11

TRI-HEXA

This is one of the simplest flexagons to be found, discovered by Arthur Stone in 1939. It uses a strip divided into equilateral triangles. The strip is joined after folding by gluing two flaps together. "Tri-Hexa" tells us the design has three faces and 6 edges.

1]

Start with the strip in this position. Fold four triangles on the left down to the right.

2]

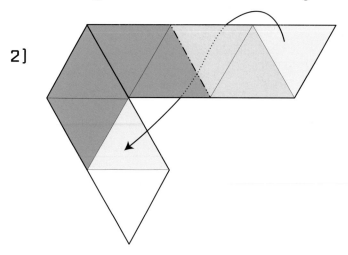

Fold the right three triangles behind and bring the last triangle in front as you fold.

3]

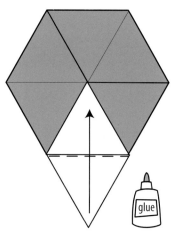

Fold the bottom triangle up and glue to its partner.

4]

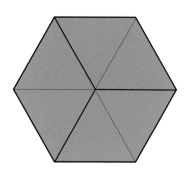

The flexagon is complete!

FLEXING:

1]

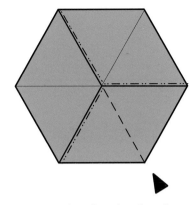

From the finished side,
emphasize these creases by
pinching them and start to
flatten the paper.

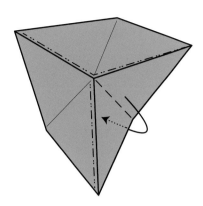

The move in progress.

2]

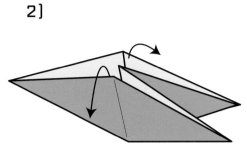

With the paper flat, ease
apart the layers to reveal
the second side.

3]

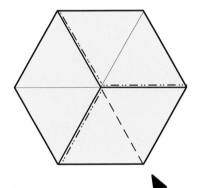

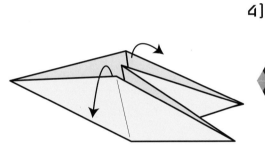

Repeat step 1.

4]

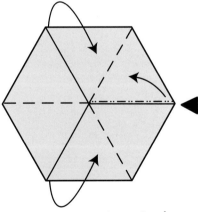

The third side is revealed.

When flexing, you can continue in the same direction, or
reverse it to show the three other sides. To do this, fold the
step backwards, ie. push the center inside to flatten, then
open out from underneath. This has a slightly smoother
"reveal" but needs little practice.

13

HEXA-HEXA

This is a development of Stone's basic Tri-Hexa design. It is the same technique, but more layers are overlapped, allowing more faces to be seen, in this case, 6.

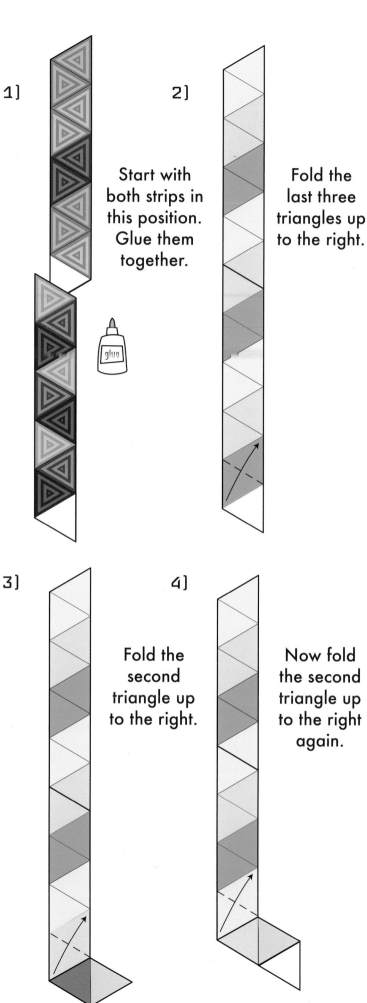

1] Start with both strips in this position. Glue them together.

2] Fold the last three triangles up to the right.

3] Fold the second triangle up to the right.

4] Now fold the second triangle up to the right again.

5]

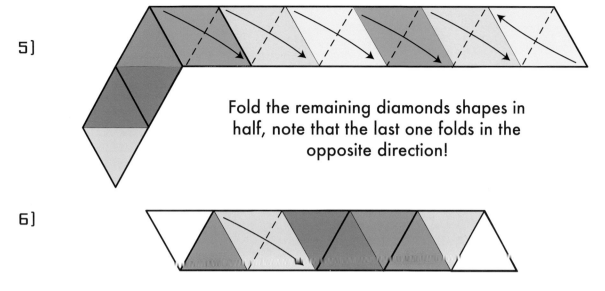

Fold the remaining diamonds shapes in half, note that the last one folds in the opposite direction!

6]

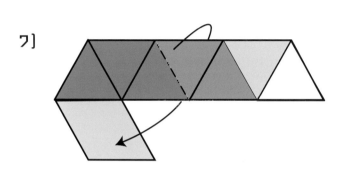

Fold the second diamond in half.

7]

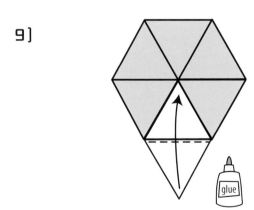

Fold the red diamond in half behind.

8]

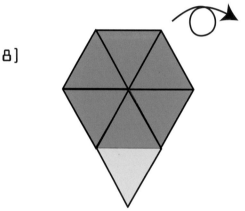

This is the result. Turn the paper over.

9]

Glue the white flaps to each other.

10]

The flexagon is complete!

FLEXING:

The design flexes in the same way as the Tri-Hexa design, though when flexing, you may not see all 6 faces /colors. To show these "hidden" faces, flex the model slightly differently by pinching on some of the faces, while pushing the on some of the faces at the same time.

INSIDE-OUT TUBE

• •

You might think it would be impossible to turn a square tube like this inside out, but through a careful series of flexes, you can do it! This flex is one that Arthur Stone created when he was part of the *Princeton Flexagon Committee*. There are several ways you can complete the transformation – see if you can discover some more.

1]

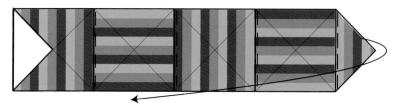

Carefully and accurately score all creases.
Fold the flat paper around into a cube shape.

2]

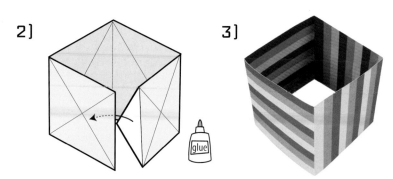

Glue the triangular flap to the inside of the other end of the shape.

3]

The model is complete.

FLEXING:

1]

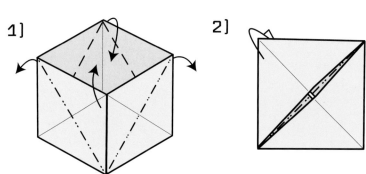

Flatten the paper using these creases.

2]

Fold the top left corner behind.

3]

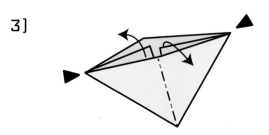

Press the sides together, folding the inner flaps in opposite directions.

4]

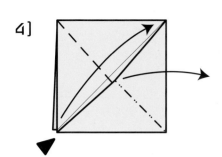

Fold the bottom left corner to the top right, squashing a triangular flap open.

5]

This is the result. Turn the paper over.

6]

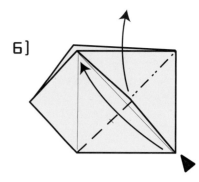

Fold the bottom right corner to the top left, squashing a triangular flap open.

7]

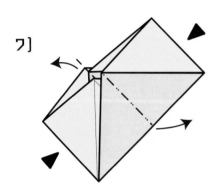

Open the model back to a tube, then squash in half in the other direction.

8]

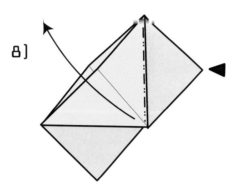

Fold the bottom right corner to the top left, squashing a triangular flap open.

9]

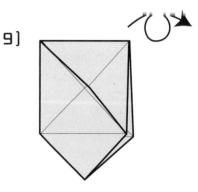

This is the result. Turn the paper over.

10]

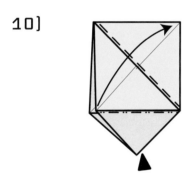

Fold the bottom left corner to the top right, squashing a triangular flap flat.

11]

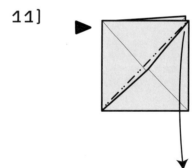

Put a finger inside from the left and open the layers evenly, folding the top corner downwards.

12]

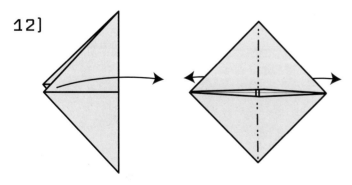

Open back out into 3D.

13]

The cycle is complete.

INSIDE-OUT CUBE

This fascinating flexagon takes the form of a cube, which is then flattened and turned completely inside out through a series of flexes. It seems impossible, even as you do it!

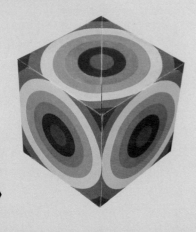

1]

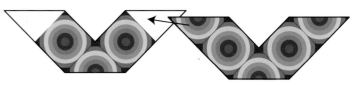

Arrange the two sections as shown, then glue the right section onto the white flap of the left section.

2]

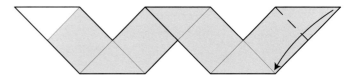

Fold down the top right triangle.

3]

Fold over on the dotted line.

4]

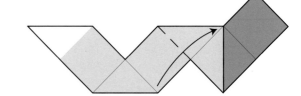

Fold over on the dotted line.

5]

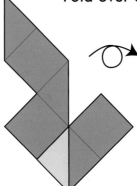

This is the result. Turn the paper over.

6]

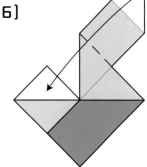

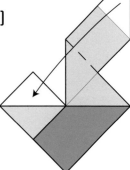

Fold over on dotted line and glue the white areas together.

7]

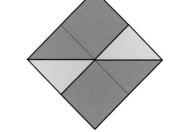

Complete.

FLEXING:

1]

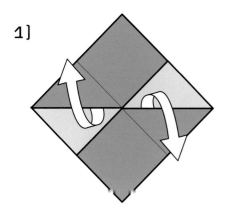

Lift up the inner green faces.

2]

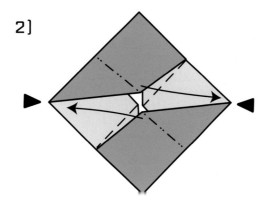

Using these crease, carefully press into a cube form and reinforce the edges to form the proper shape.

3]

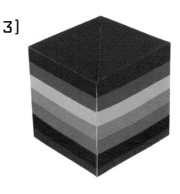

Flatten back to step 1.

4]

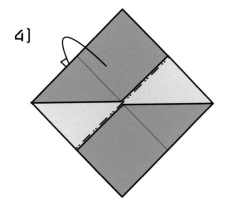

Fold the upper left half underneath.

5]

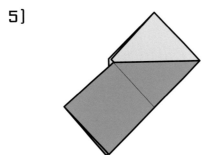

Fold down the green flap to the lower right.

6]

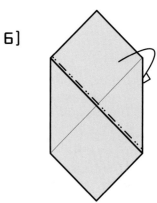

Fold the upper right half underneath.

7]

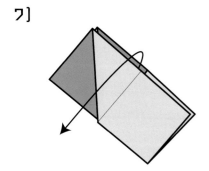

Fold the blue flap to the lower left.

8]

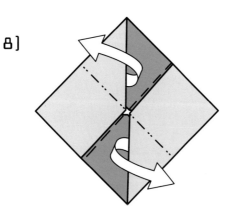

Open as in step 2.

9]

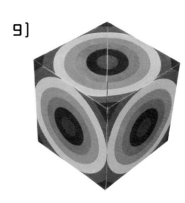

The inverted cube!

HOLLOW RING KALEIDO

This model is a simplified version of the Hexagonal Ring Kaleidocycle, where one of the faces is left out, so that you can open up hidden colors almost like opening the petals of a flower. Try flexing it in both directions to see the full range of transformations.

1]

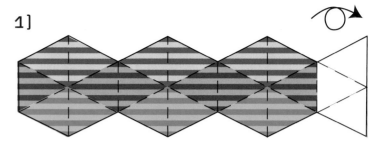

Score all the creases. Turn the paper over.

2]

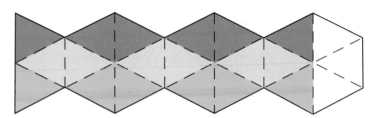

Score the same creases.

3]

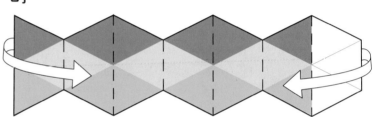

Fold the sides around to form the model into 3D.

4]

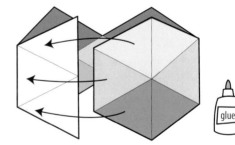

Glue the colored flaps onto the white area.

5]

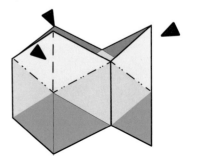

Allow the glue to set, then fold the top level corners towards the center of the model.

6]

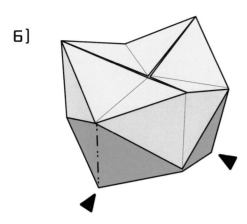

Push in the lower corners in, and pinch the paper to move it toward the center on top and bottm.

7]

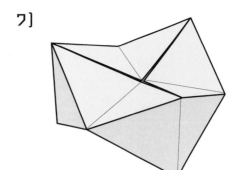

Ready for flexing.

FLEXING:

1]

Flex the corners to the center.

2]

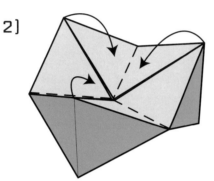

Again, flex the corners to the center.

3]

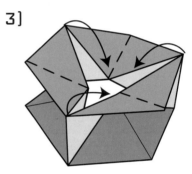

The hollow sides of the shape are revealed. Flex three corners towards the center again.

4]

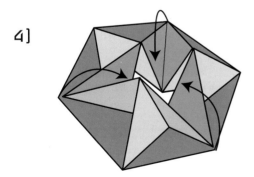

Here is an intermediate stage, where some beautiful "petal" like flaps are on display.

5]

Keep flexing and you will return to the start again.

HEXAGONAL RING KALEIDO

This is a three-dimensional, hexagonal design which flexes in upon itself, allowing continuous rotation of the model, while revealing the various combinations of faces.

1]

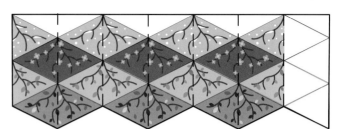

Score these creases. Turn the paper over.

2]

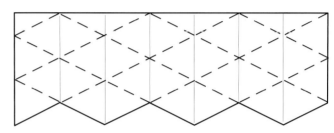

Score these creases.

3]

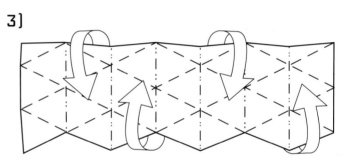

Begin to form the model into 3D by rolling the long sides toward each other.

4]

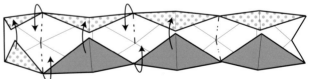

Glue the green flaps onto the patterned flaps by bringing the lower flaps up and under the corresponding upper flaps.

5]

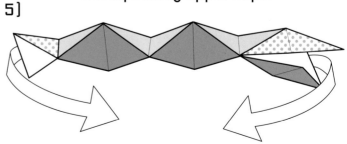

Allow the glue to set, then bring the two sides toward each other to form a ring.

6]

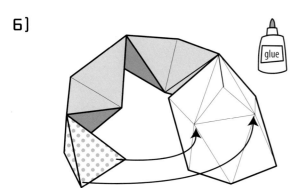

Feed one end inside the other
and glue in place.

7]

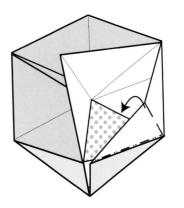

Glue this flap down

8]

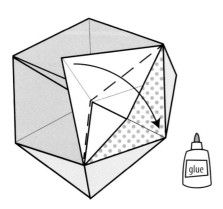

Fold the final flap down, gluing
it into place.

9]

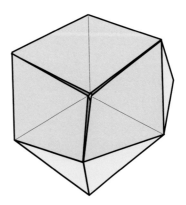

Complete.

FLEXING:

1]

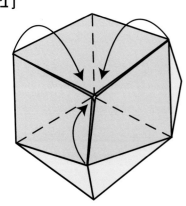

Face 1. Flex the corners
to the center.

2]

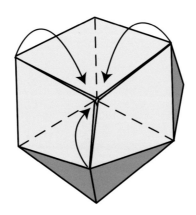

Face 2. Flex the corners
to the center.

3]

Face 3. Continue until you
are fully relaxed.

OCTAGONAL RING KALEIDO

By extending the length of the Hexagonal Ring Kaleidocycle, we can create an octagonal form. Being looser in structure, you can press various sides together to produce different shapes, as well as the normal flexing.

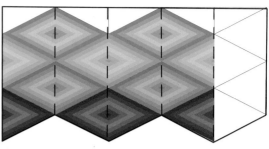

1]

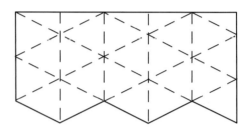

Cut out the two halves and score these creases. Turn the paper over.

2]

Score these creases.

3]

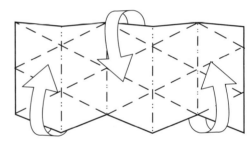

Begin to form the model into 3D by bringing the lower flaps up and under the corresponding upper flaps.

4]

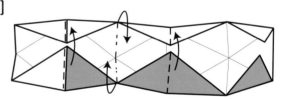

Glue the lower level flaps (including half of two patterns) onto the upper level flaps.

5]

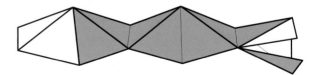

Allow the glue to set, then make the second ring base in the same way.

6]

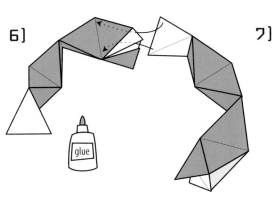

Add glue inside all the faces of the open end of the left half, then feed the end of the right half inside and press all layers firmly in place as the glue sets.

7]

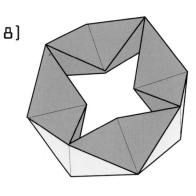

Join the open ends together in the same way.

8]

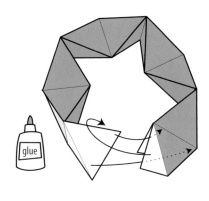

This is the result.

FLEXING:

1]

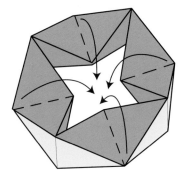

Fold the outer corners to the middle.

2]

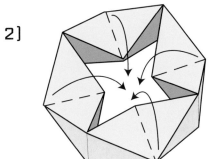

Repeat.

3]

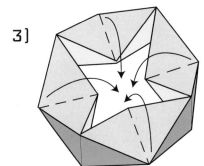

Repeat.

4]

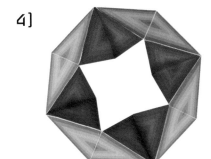

Here is the final color combination.

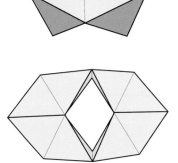

Here are some other shapes you can create. Can you find others?

CUBE KALEIDOCYCLE

This is an eye-catching model which seems to expand and collapse in an unexpected fashion, opening to huge capacity and closing completely shut.

1]

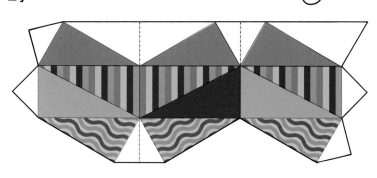

Cut along outline and score creases. Cut on dotted lines as shown. Turn paper over.

2]

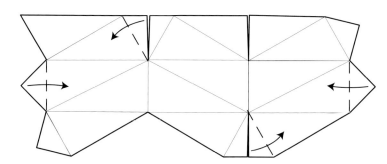

Fold these flaps over.

3]

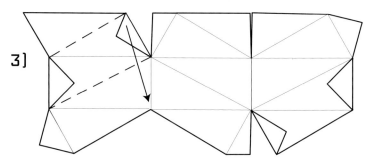

Fold the left-hand side in on itself.

4]

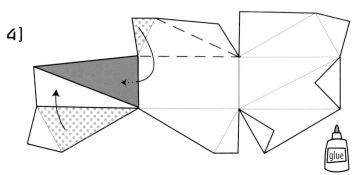

Glue the lower left flap onto the adjoining surface. Glue the small flap into the pocket.

5]

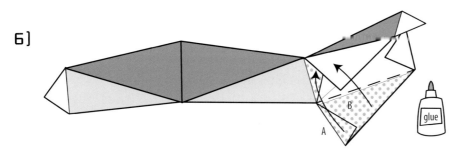

Glue these two flaps onto the adjoining surface.

6]

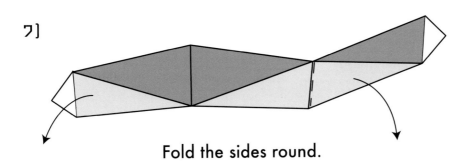

A: Glue the small triangles together.
B. Glue the lower flap on top of the upper.

7]

Fold the sides round.

8]

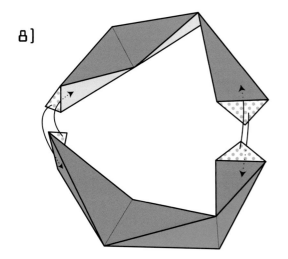

Make the other section. Add glue to all
the flaps then interlock the two halves
(squeeze the sides sightly to open them).

FLEXING:

Simply rotate the model and enjoy
the beauty of its flexing movement.

HEXA-FLIPPER

This design has a number of flexing permutations and it is important to score as precisely as you can. Try also not to add glue outside the white areas! The diagram looks a lot more complicated than this actually is, and its rotation is one of the most fascinating and soothing to build.

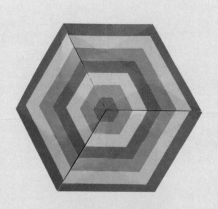

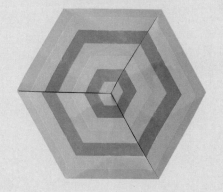

1]

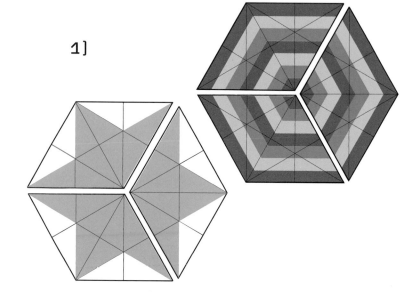

Arrange the pieces as shown.

2]

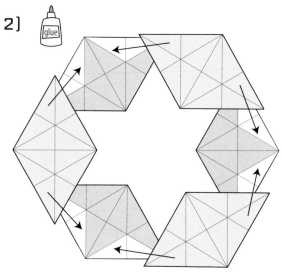

On the solid pattern, glue the geometric pattern to the triangles with arrowheads, carefully noting that the 2nd white triangle is unglued.

3]

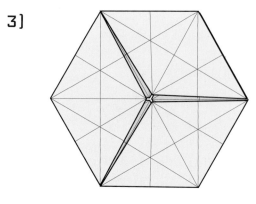

Complete!

FLEXING:

1]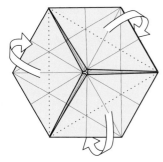

Fold three corners behind along creases shown by dotted lines.

2]

Lift up the inner corners and fold them to the outer corners, pressing the sides in as you do.

3]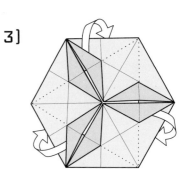

Fold back the hidden corners underneath the diamonds.

4]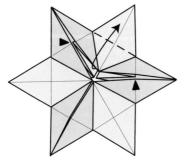

Fold an inner corner out, allowing layers to open out.

5]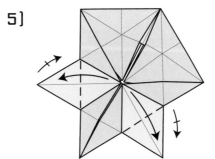

This is the result. Repeat on two other corners.

6]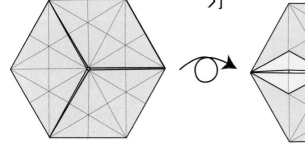

This is the result. Turn the paper over.

7]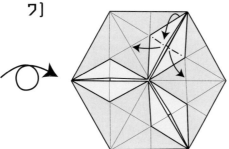

Fold the corners inward, opening out two layers.

8]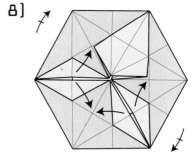

This is the result. Repeat on two other corners.

9]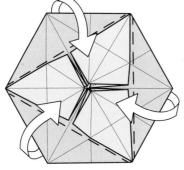

Fold the outside corners to the center.

10]

Complete.

FLEXICUBE

This fascinating flexagon takes the form of a cube, which is then flattened and turned completely inside out through a series of flexes. Lined up in formation, stacked in a row or squared up into one giant cube, it seems impossible even as you create it! Just keep turning!

1]

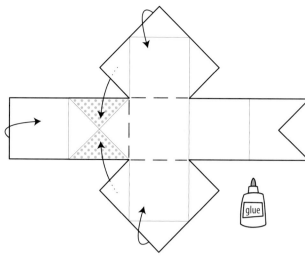

Cut out the shapes, arrange as shown and fold three sides upward. Glue the side flaps to the central flap.

2]

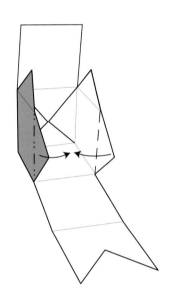

Fold the triangular flaps inward.

3]

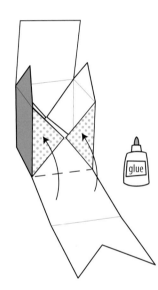

Lift up the central flap and glue the sides to it.

4]

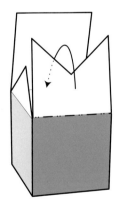

Fold the central flap inward.

5]

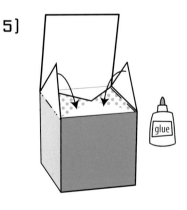

Glue the side flaps to the central flap. Put your finger in the hole to press the layers together while they set.

6]

Glue the final flap into place.

ASSEMBLING:

1]

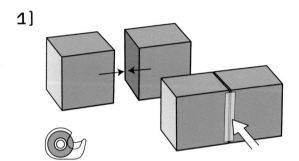

Arrange two cubes like this and apply a tape hinge.

3]

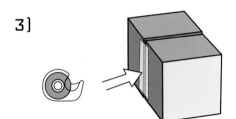

Apply a tape hinge on the left. Repeat assembly steps 1 through 3, creating a 2nd set of taped cubes.

5]

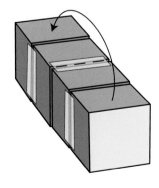

Fold the nearest two cubes up and onto the other two. Duplicate these four, following steps 1 through 5.

7]

Complete. Repeat with the seven other cubes.

2]

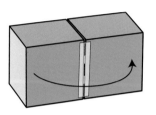

Fold the left cube around to lie on the right cube.

4]

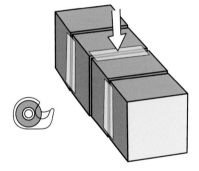

Arrange the two cubes like this and add a tape hinge in the center.

6]

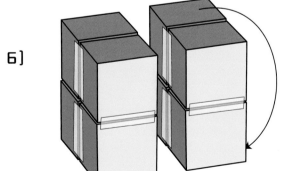

Flip the second set of cubes 180°.

7]

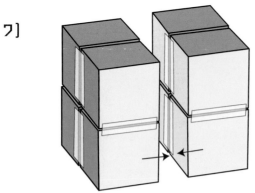

Bring both sets together as shown (same color faces toward each other).

8]

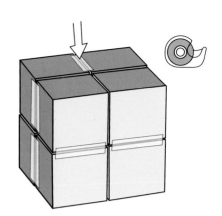

Add a tape hinge to the rear center.

9]

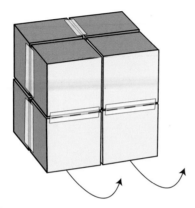

Fold out the lower half.

10]

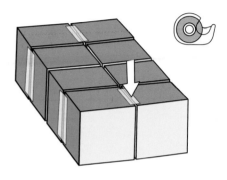

Add a tape hinge to the near center.

11]

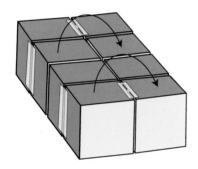

Fold the left half on top of the right half.

12]

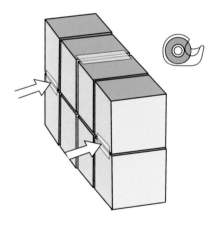

Add two hinges where shown.

13]

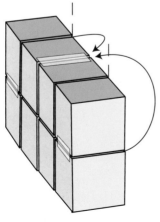

Fold the front and rear sections to lie on the left side.

13]

This assembly will mezmerize you as you flex and turn it upon itself!

FOR ALL PATTERNS, CUT ALONG THE EDGES OF THE ARTWORK.

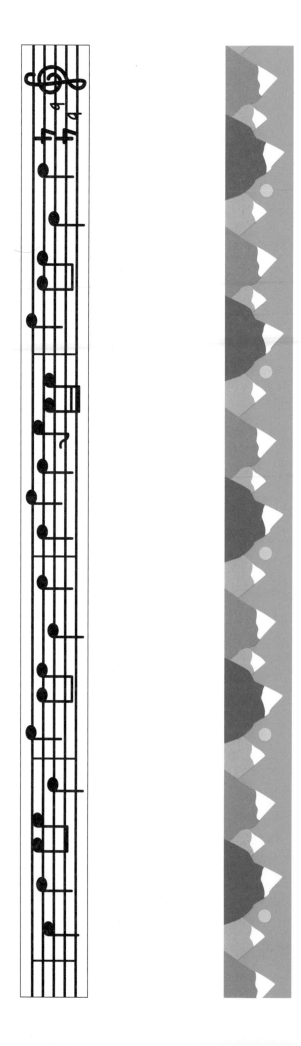

FOR ALL PATTERNS, CUT ALONG THE EDGES OF THE ARTWORK.

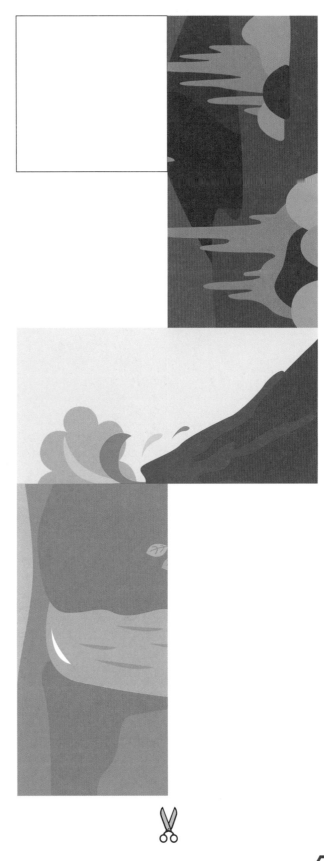

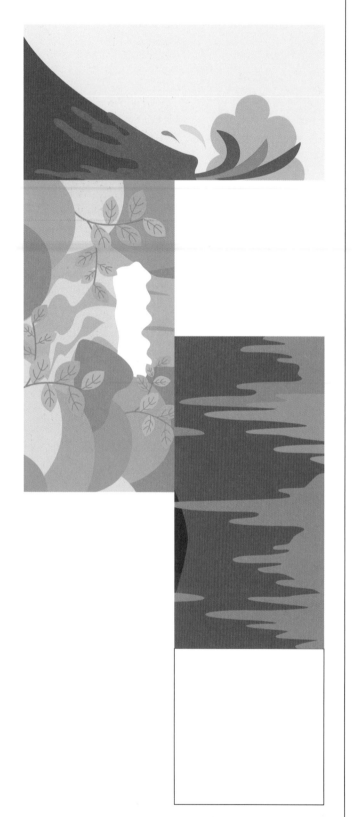

For all patterns, cut along the edges of the artwork and cut along any dotted lines inside the patterns.

FOR ALL PATTERNS, CUT ALONG THE EDGES OF THE ARTWORK
AND CUT ALONG ANY DOTTED LINES INSIDE THE PATTERNS.

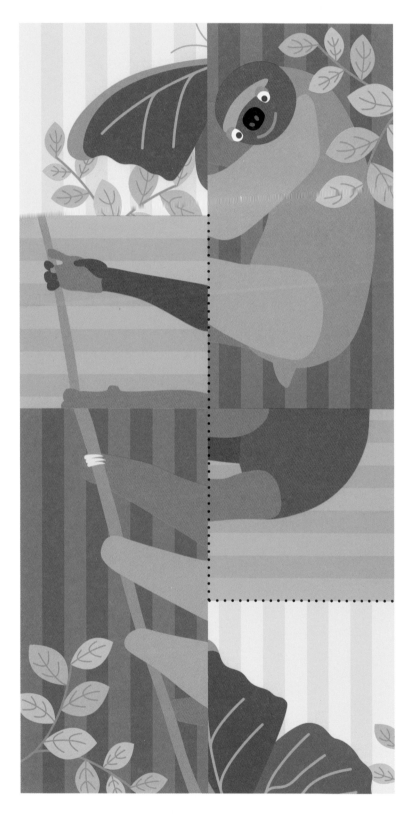

FOR ALL PATTERNS, CUT ALONG THE EDGES OF THE ARTWORK
AND CUT ALONG ANY DOTTED LINES INSIDE THE PATTERNS.

FOR ALL PATTERNS, CUT ALONG THE EDGES OF THE ARTWORK
AND CUT ALONG ANY DOTTED LINES INSIDE THE PATTERNS.

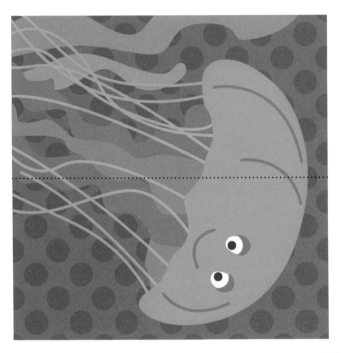

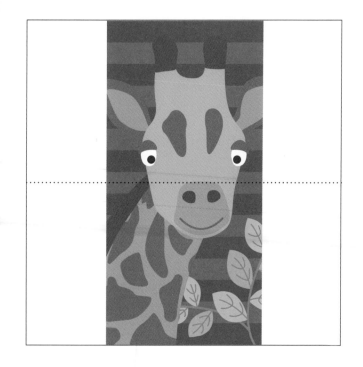

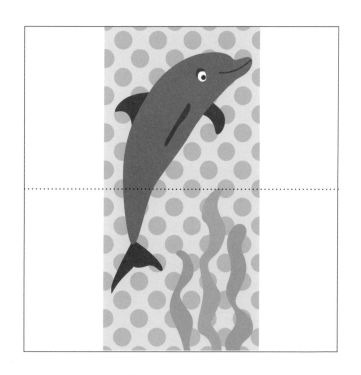

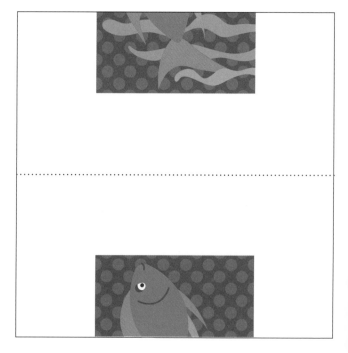

FOR ALL PATTERNS, CUT ALONG THE EDGES OF THE ARTWORK.

(COLOR IN THE PATTERN)

FOR ALL PATTERNS, CUT ALONG THE EDGES OF THE ARTWORK.

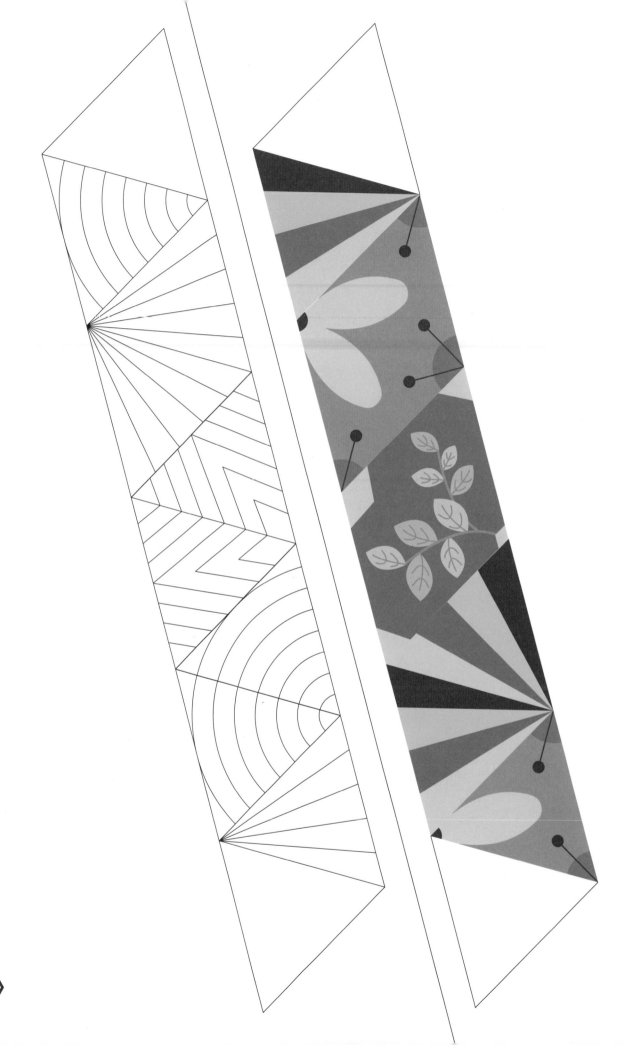

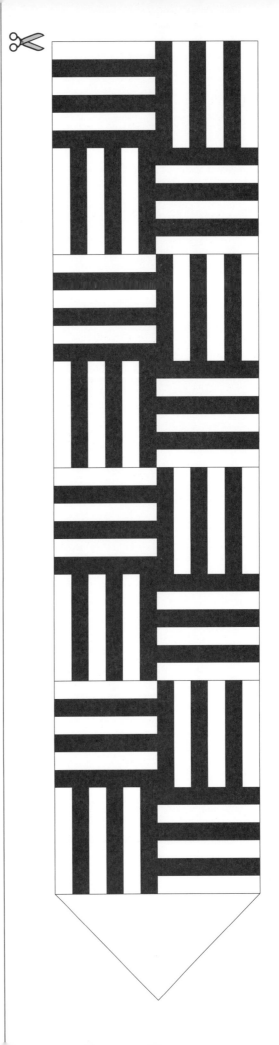

(COLOR IN THE PATTERN)

FOR ALL PATTERNS, CUT ALONG THE EDGES OF THE ARTWORK.

FOR ALL PATTERNS, CUT ALONG THE EDGES OF THE ARTWORK.

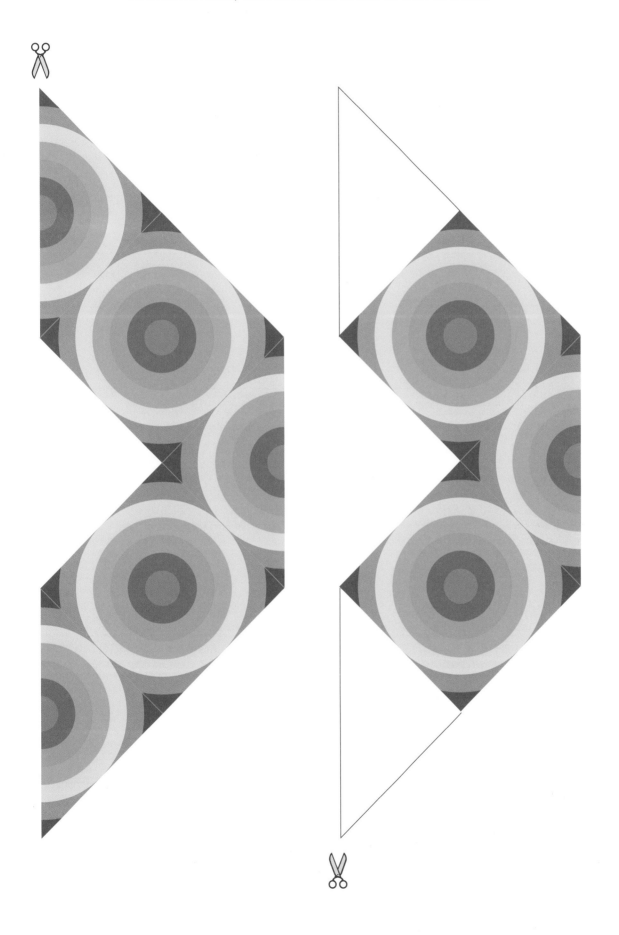

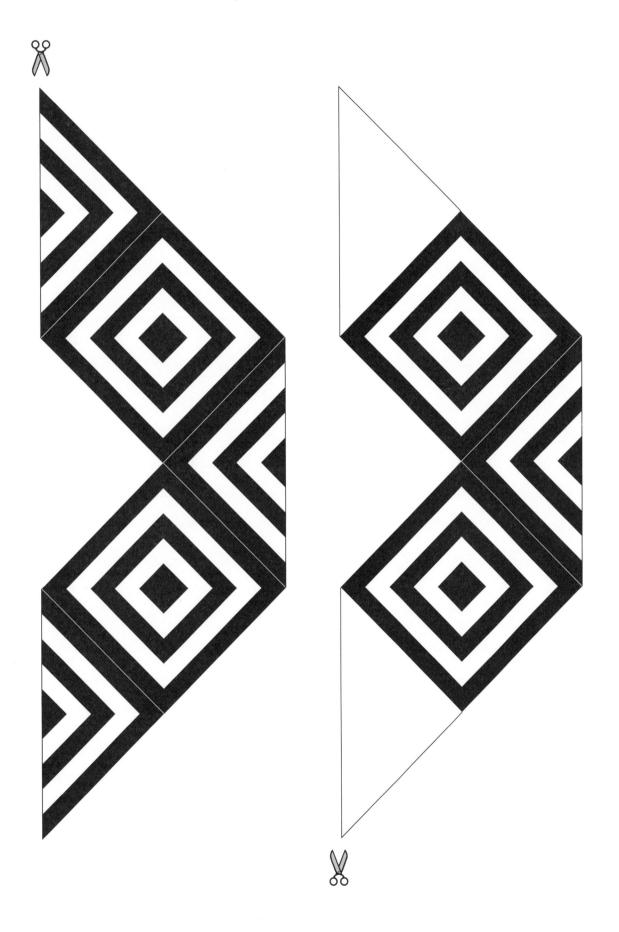

FOR ALL PATTERNS, CUT ALONG THE EDGES OF THE ARTWORK.

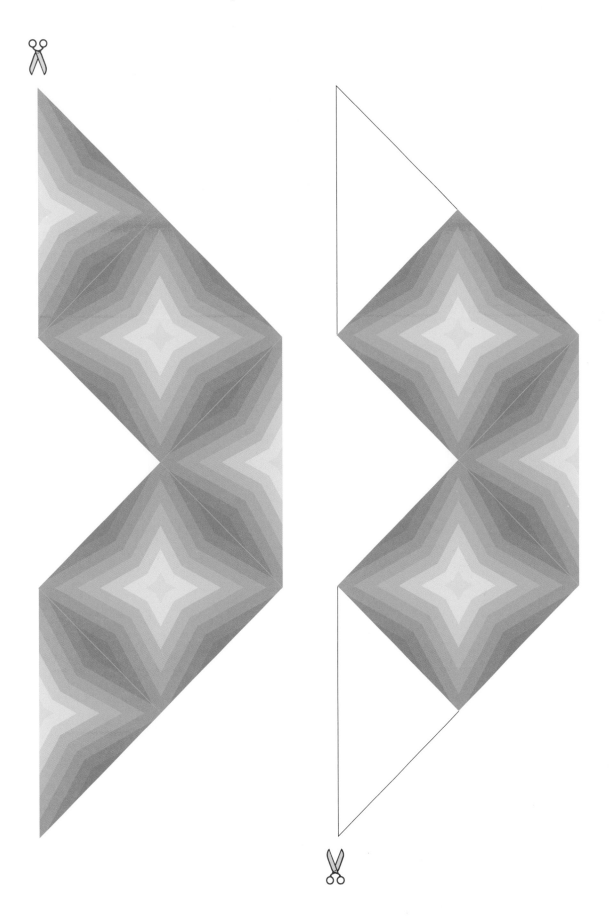

FOR ALL PATTERNS, CUT ALONG THE EDGES OF THE ARTWORK.

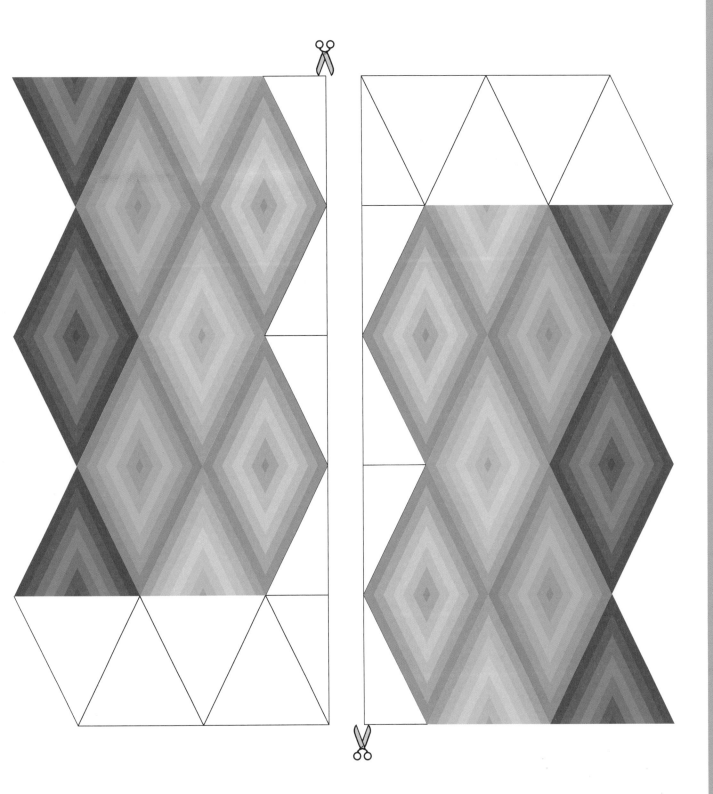

FOR ALL PATTERNS, CUT ALONG THE EDGES OF THE ARTWORK.

FOR ALL PATTERNS, CUT ALONG THE EDGES OF THE ARTWORK.

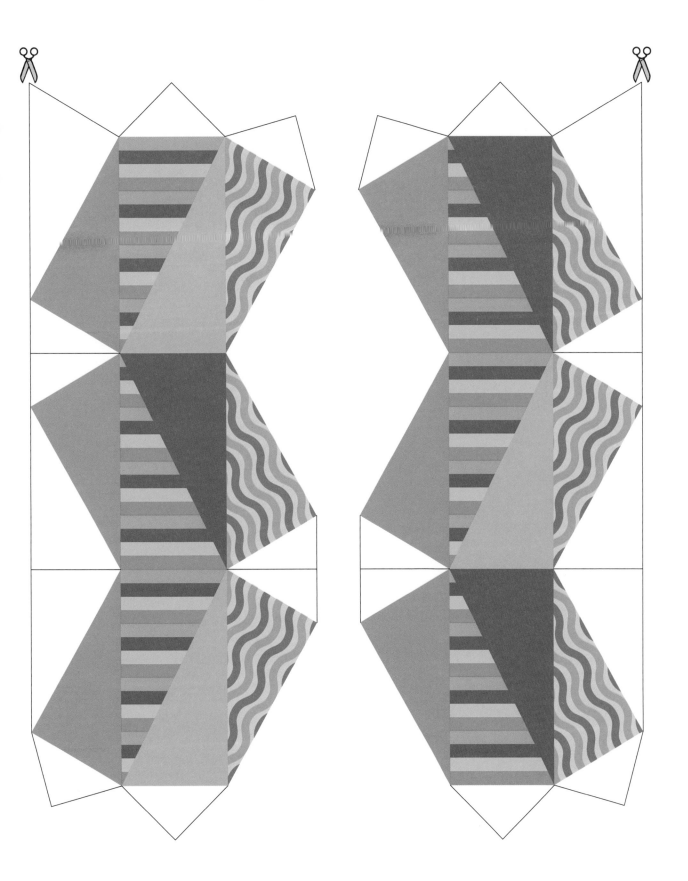

FOR ALL PATTERNS, CUT ALONG THE EDGES OF THE ARTWORK.

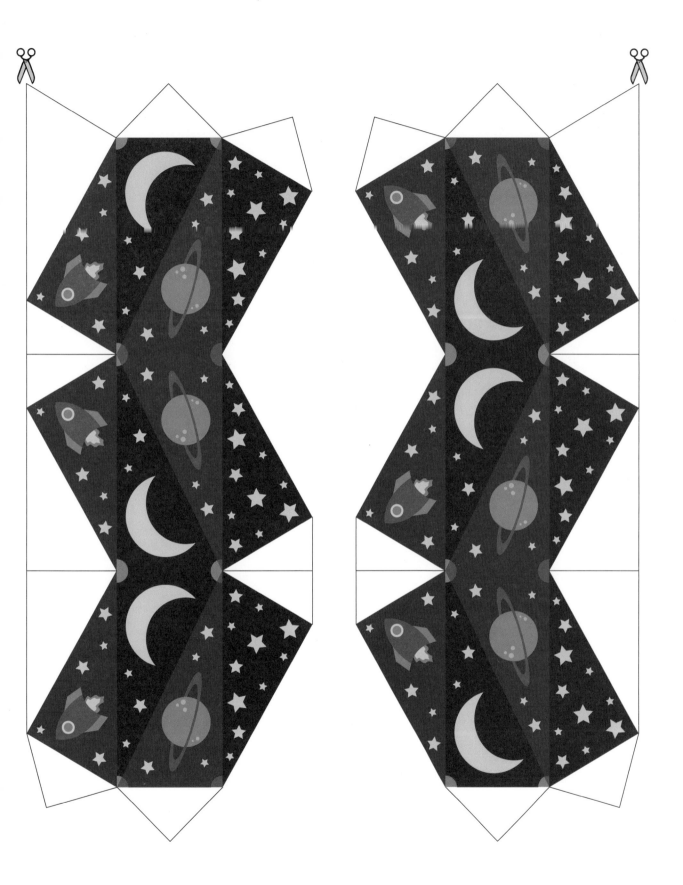

(COLOR IN THE PATTERN)

FOR ALL PATTERNS, CUT ALONG THE EDGES OF THE ARTWORK.

FOR ALL PATTERNS, CUT ALONG THE EDGES OF THE ARTWORK.

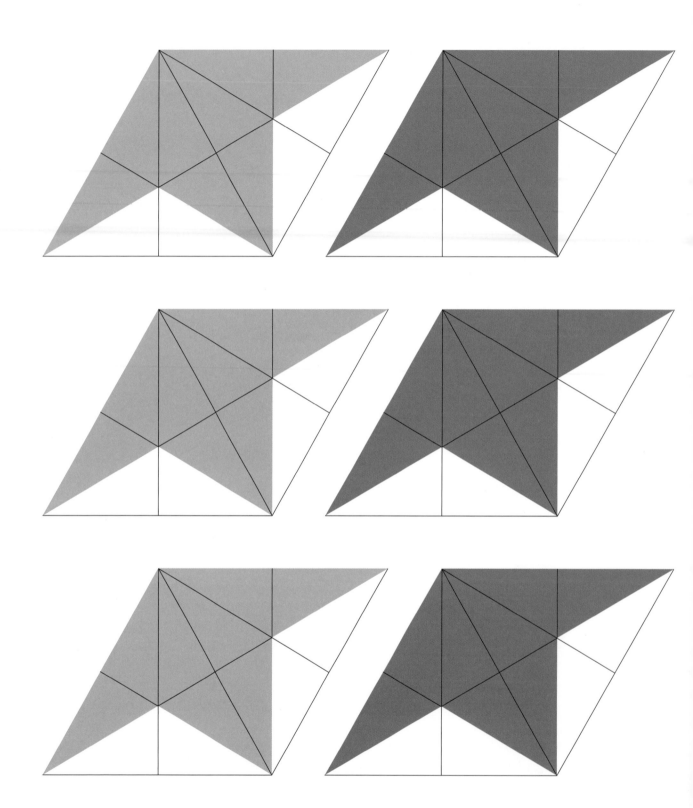

FOR ALL PATTERNS, CUT ALONG THE EDGES OF THE ARTWORK.

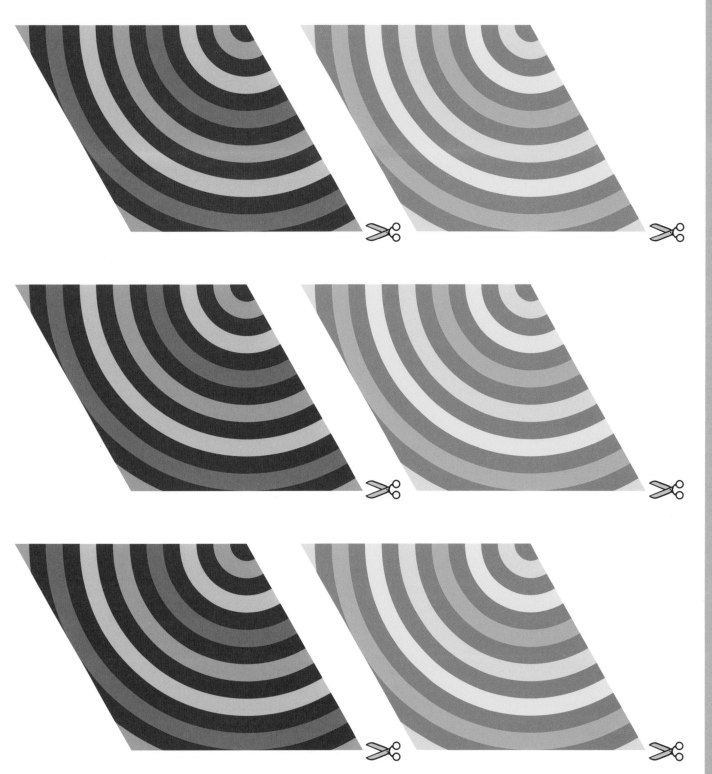

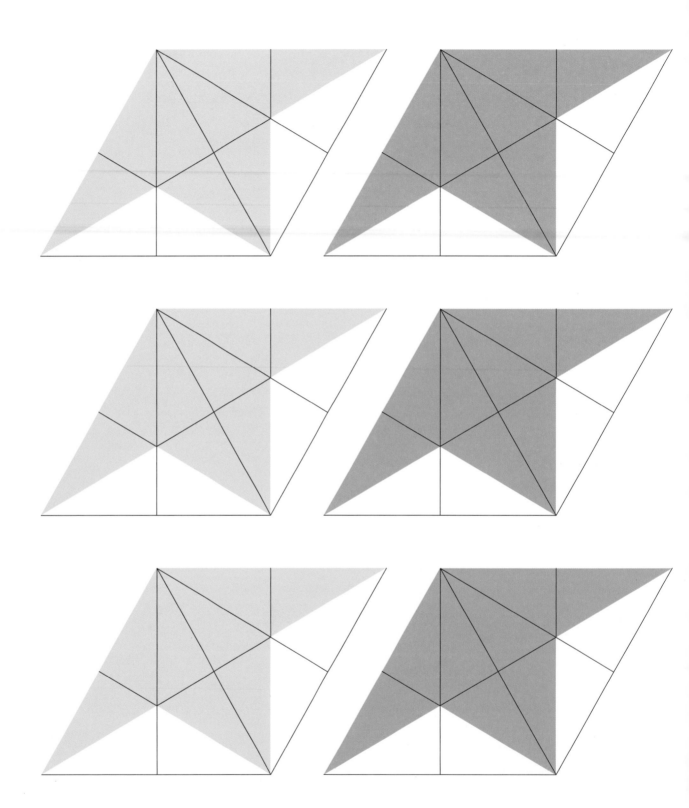

FOR ALL PATTERNS,
CUT ALONG THE EDGES
OF THE ARTWORK.

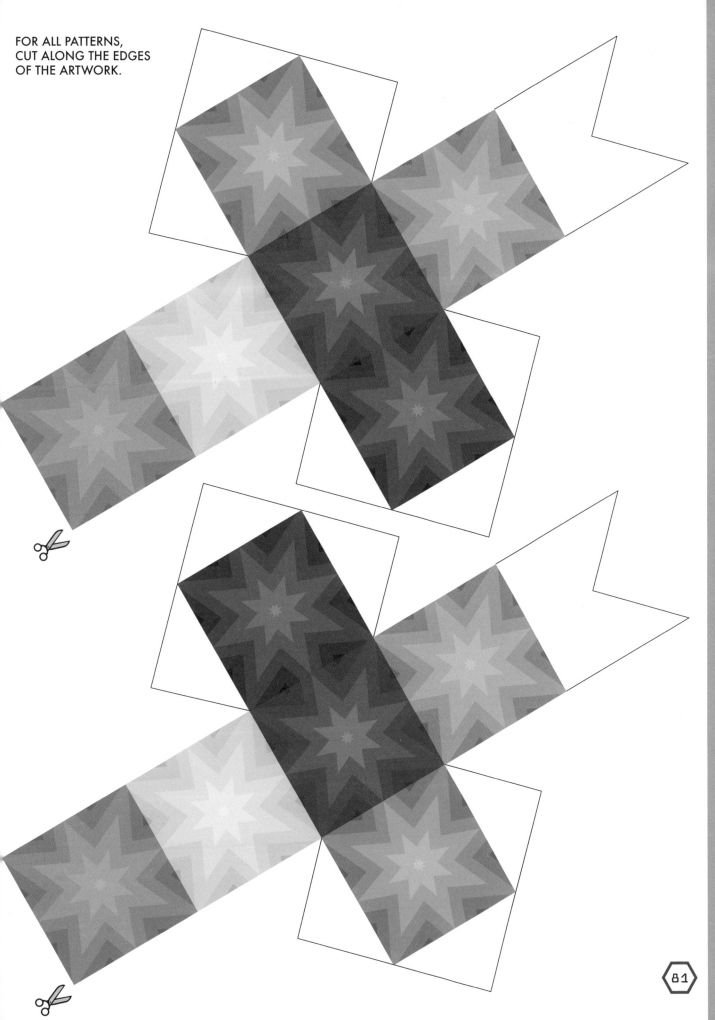

FOR ALL PATTERNS,
CUT ALONG THE EDGES
OF THE ARTWORK.

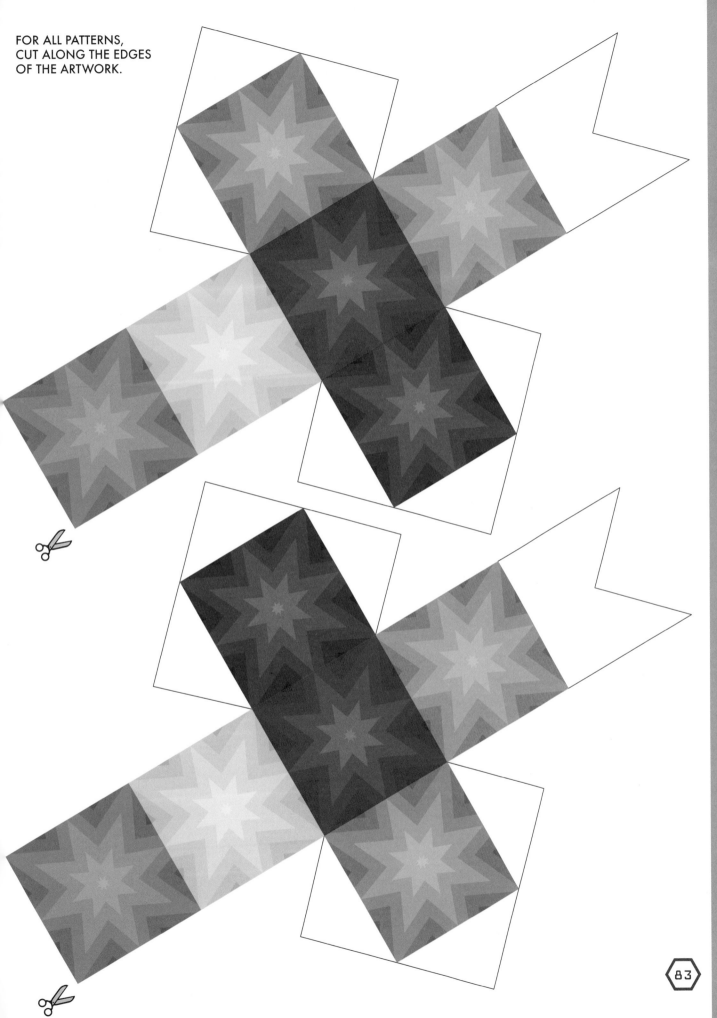

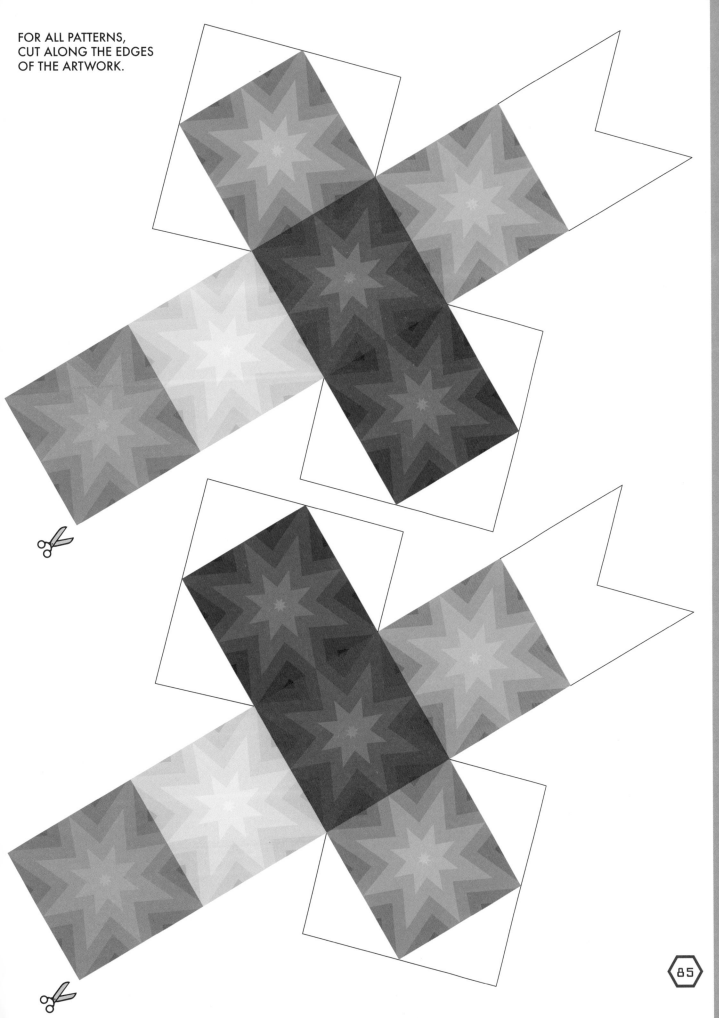

FOR ALL PATTERNS,
CUT ALONG THE EDGES
OF THE ARTWORK.

FOR ALL PATTERNS,
CUT ALONG THE EDGES
OF THE ARTWORK.

FOR ALL PATTERNS,
CUT ALONG THE EDGES
OF THE ARTWORK.

FOR ALL PATTERNS,
CUT ALONG THE EDGES
OF THE ARTWORK.

FOR ALL PATTERNS,
CUT ALONG THE EDGES
OF THE ARTWORK.

FOR ALL PATTERNS,
CUT ALONG THE EDGES
OF THE ARTWORK.